SPOTLIGHT ON SPECIAL EDUCATIONAL NEEDS: PHYSICAL DISABILITIES

Contents

Acknowledgements

The author and publishers wish to express their gratitude to:

- June Pollard for her tireless efforts in typing the manuscript;

- John Voice, Headteacher of Filsham Valley School, for his advice and support;

- Mike Phillips, Filsham Valley School, for the photographic work;

- Parents and pupils of the Centre facility (Filsham Valley School) for their help and contributions.

SPOTLIGHT ON SPECIAL EDUCATIONAL NEEDS:
PHYSICAL DISABILITIES

Preface

Integration, or 'inclusion' as it is more increasingly termed, has become a major focus in recent years following the *Education Act, 1981*'s recognition that most children with special educational needs would be educated in mainstream schools.

When the term integration is used in connection with special needs, it implies an environment where pupils with such needs are educated alongside their peers.

The Warnock Report (1978) identified three main forms of integration: locational, social and functional. Locational integration describes a special unit or class set up in mainstream school, or a situation where a special school and mainstream school share the same site. Social integration is described as being where children who attend a special class or unit, play with other children at the school and spend extra-curricular time with them. Functional integration describes the fullest form of integration and consists of a school in which social and locational integration combine. In other words, when children with special educational needs join part time or full time in the regular classes of the mainstream school, and socialise with them at all other times.

This booklet is concerned with *functional integration* and how it can be achieved for students with physical disabilities. While Tilstone (1995) stated that 'there is evidence to suggest that pupils with even the most severe disabilities are beginning to take their rightful place in local communities', it is recognised here that the majority of mainstream schools are not yet ready to cater for such pupils and so it attempts to enable schools to respond flexibly to pupils with a range of more commonly encountered disabilities. Strategies are suggested which can enable pupils with or without a statement to gain access to the full National Curriculum. Some of the issues involved in responding to the *Code of Practice, 1994* are addressed, notably the identification, assessment and provision for pupils with physical disabilities, together with some ideas for the writing of individual education plans.

Responding to the Code of Practice

Identification and Assessment

The *Code of Practice* offers guidance on the staged approach to the identification and assessment of special educational needs of pupils in schools. The guidance embodies principles which are central to the *Code* and to which all schools should have regard. In assessing the nature of the exceptional special educational needs of a student with physical disabilities at any stage, schools should:

- ensure that provision matches the student's needs;

- carefully record the special educational needs, action taken and the outcome;

- consider the wishes and feelings of the child;

- consult and act in partnership with the parents;

- involve an outside specialist in the stage preceding referral to LEA for statutory assessment.

In order to identify and assess needs, it is necessary for a special educational needs co-ordinator (SENCO) to consider the educational implications of the student's disability.

Educational Implications of Disabilities

In order for the integration of pupils with physical disabilities to succeed, teachers' understanding of the special needs of each student is essential, both for the relevance to teaching and for the impact on attitudes of teachers. Medical labels however, are not always helpful as there can be a very wide range of abilities within each condition. It should also be remembered that many children have a combination of conditions and may, in addition, have associated behavioural, learning and/or psychological disorders. For example, a child who is comparatively able-bodied may have quite severe learning difficulties associated with his/her condition. Alternatively, a student who is severely disabled may require less support if they are well-adjusted, than a less disabled pupil who finds it difficult to cope with his/her disability. Teachers should therefore always be aware of the frequent overlap between medical, social, psychological and educational implications.

Physical condition/disability

Learning ability

Emotional/behavioural state

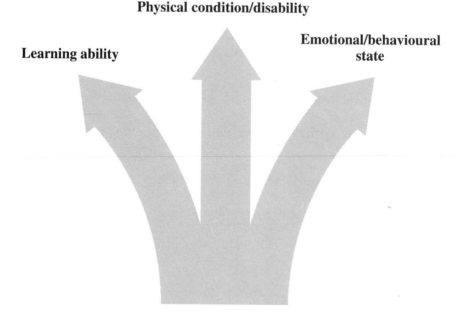

Figure 1 – There is frequent overlap between medical, social, psychological and educational implications.

Biological knowledge of a child's disability is, by itself, no guide to what the child is like. Additionally it is possible for teachers to become overly fascinated in a child's physical condition, so that the child as an individual is overshadowed by the disability. The information that most teachers need to know prior to teaching a student with a physical disability is:

- will s/he have learning difficulties?

- will s/he use a wheelchair?

- will s/he require adapted technical aids?

- what symptoms, if any, do I need to recognise in case of emergencies?

It is important to emphasise that teachers do not need to be medical experts on each type of disability. There should be adequate information available, but most teachers need to be concerned with the *educational implications of disability* only.

The following summaries outline a brief description of types of physical disability, their causes and the education implications which are, for the majority of mainstream teachers, the overriding concern. It should be noted, however, that they are general comments only. Pupils with the same disability rarely have identical needs, and provision should therefore plan for *individuals*.

Cerebral Palsy

Description

Cerebral palsy is a disorder which is caused by damage to a developing brain. The brain damage that causes cerebral palsy can also produce a number of other disabilities. There are various forms of cerebral palsy: spasticity (disordered control of movement), athetosis (frequent involuntary movements) and ataxia (unsteady gait with balance problems).

Effects range from changed muscle tone to quadriplegia, where all four limbs and the total body are affected. No two children with this condition are affected in the same way. Some have only slight disability while others may have severe multiple disabilities which include communication problems, learning difficulties, hearing impairment and epilepsy. All have problems with *movement and posture.*

Causes

Cerebral palsy can be caused by a variety of diseases, before and after birth, or labour and/or delivery, asphyxia, premature birth and brain injury.

Educational Implications

Co-ordination – Some children have poor fine and gross motor skills, which can have an effect on handwriting and physical education. Practical work in classrooms may also be affected by involuntary movements.

Learning difficulties – Pupils with cerebral palsy commonly have spatial and/or perceptional difficulties.

Communication – Some pupils have difficulty with speaking due to lack of control of the muscles of the mouth. Advice and/or treatment from a speech therapist may be necessary.

Fatigue – Pupils with more severe forms of cerebral palsy tire easily.

Mobility – Pupils may have limited mobility and may use walking aids or wheelchairs, which have implications for space and access to buildings. They may require additional time to get around the school to classrooms, assembly areas and sports facilities.

Personal care – Some pupils with cerebral palsy may need help with toileting arrangements and/or dressing. They may require additional time to change. They may need help to eat meals. Therefore, they may require ancillary support at such times.

Pastoral support – Pupils may experience emotional problems and frustration associated with their disability. They may therefore require extra pastoral time.

Spina Bifida

Description
The term spina bifida refers to a separation in the bones of the spinal column, exposing nerves. Physical consequences depend on the lesion and the amount of damage to the spinal cord. This can result in minimal or complete paralysis below the level of the lesion. Bowel and bladder control may be affected.

Causes
The cause of spina bifida is unclear, but is believed to include environmental and genetic factors. Once a child with spina bifida has been born to a family, the risk to further pregnancies is increased.

Educational Implications
Learning difficulties – Spatial and/or perceptual problems are common. There is frequently a language problem in that there is a considerable difference between the level of verbal performance and intellectual ability. Comprehension frequently does not match reading ability. Students with

spina bifida can be fluent talkers and may give the impression that they understand without doing so. Speech therapy advice and/or treatment may therefore be necessary.

Motor and spatial problems may cause difficulties with number work and handwriting.

Concentration span may be poor.

Co-ordination – Some pupils have poor motor skills which may affect practical tasks, physical education and handwriting.

Organisation – Many children with spina bifida have difficulties in ordering and organising materials.

Mobility – Some pupils with spina bifida may use a wheelchair or walking aids. This may have implications for access to buildings and space in classrooms and corridors. Additional time may be needed to get to lessons.

Personal care – Pupils with spina bifida may need help with access to toilet facilities and/or dressing. They may require additional time to make such arrangements and/or ancillary support at such times.

Hydrocephalus

Description

Hydrocephalus is a condition in which the ventricles in the brain are enlarged, as a result of obstructed flow of cerebral spinal fluid. It is commonly associated with spina bifida, so that educational implications may be similar.

Generally, children with hydrocephalus require a bypass, or shunting procedure, so that the fluid from the brain can be diverted into the abdominal cavity. A plastic catheter is inserted into one of the enlarged ventricles and is connected to another catheter that is placed into the skin behind the child's ear. This catheter runs under the skin of the neck and chest and into the abdominal cavity. Extra tubing is left in the abdomen, so that as a child grows, the tubing can uncoil without getting clogged.

Causes

The cause of hydrocephalus is unclear, but is thought to be linked to certain environmental and genetic factors.

Educational Implications
Medical – The shunt may become blocked or infected, which can be life-threatening. Teachers will therefore need to be aware of symptoms, so that medical treatment may be sought immediately. They are:

- severe headache;

- vomiting;

- irritability.

Associated conditions – Children with hydrocephalus may also have other complications such as seizures, decreased mobility, and cognitive delay or deficits.

Learning difficulties – Pupils may have varying degrees of learning difficulties. Spatial and/or perceptual problems are common. Number work can cause difficulties and memory may be poor.

Organisation – Many children with hydrocephalus have difficulties in ordering and organising equipment.

Muscular Dystrophy

Description
There are several types of muscular dystrophy, which are all progressive diseases, resulting in breakdown of muscle fibre and gradually increasing muscle weakness. Some types affect both sexes, but the most common form is Duchene muscular dystrophy which affects only boys. The muscle weakness progresses slowly and there are times of remission as well as rapid deterioration. The life expectancy of pupils with muscular dystrophy is limited and some die in their late teens.

Educational Implications
Mobility – The nature of the disease means that all provision must include *anticipated decreased* mobility. This will have implications for access to buildings, space in rooms and provision for social trips. The use of a wheelchair is necessary at a later stage of the disease.

Motor control – The disease particularly affects hands and arms. Handwriting and practical tasks may therefore be affected, and additional technical aids may be necessary.

Absence from school – In the later stages, illness may become more frequent and result in increased absence. Staff and pupils will also need to be prepared for the possibility of the death of a pupil still of school age.

Varying degrees of disability – There can be long periods of remission, when less support is necessary, together with rapid deterioration at other times, requiring extra help. A *flexible and rapid* response to aid is therefore essential.

Pastoral support – Pupils with muscular dystrophy become more dependent for daily care needs during adolescence, at a time when most other pupils become more independent. This requires additional pastoral help and sensitive awareness by all staff. Careers guidance should also be carefully considered.

Special arrangements – Additional time and/or an amanuensis may be necessary for exams and tests, due to muscle fatigue. Special arrangements will need to be negotiated with the Examining Board.

Personal care – Students at an advanced stage of muscular dystrophy may require help with access to toilet facilities or with practical tasks such as eating. They may therefore require ancillary support for some part of the day.

Spinal Curvatures

Description
There are three main types of spinal curvatures: Scoliosis, Kyphosis and Lordosis. They all affect posture and mobility. Scoliosis is a lateral curvature of the spine, where one shoulder blade is more prominent and one hip is higher than the other. Lordosis describes a forward curvature of the spine, as viewed from the side. Kyphosis is a posterior curvature of the spine, affecting lung capacity in severe cases and shortened stature.

Causes
Spinal curvatures are usually caused by congenital or neuromuscular disorders, such as spina bifida, cerebral palsy or muscular dystrophy. They can also develop as a result of tumours, infections and metabolic diseases.

Educational Implications

Pain – Pupils may experience continuous pain and this may affect their ability to concentrate.

Mobility – Impaired mobility may result in the inability to participate in most PE activities, or outdoor trips.

Posture – Sitting in a regular school chair may become very difficult if the condition is left untreated.

Pastoral support – Some pupils may have low self-esteem, related to self-image. They may need to wear a body brace or jacket to correct posture, as advised by the health service. This may lead to teasing. Additional pastoral support will therefore be necessary.

Limb Deficiencies

Description

Pupils may have partial or total limb deficiency. When children are born with a limb deficiency, they may have sensitivity in the remaining section of the limb.

Causes

Limb deficiencies may be congenital or acquired.

The cause of congenital limb deficiencies is not known. Only a very small percentage show a hereditary link. Following the banning of the drug thalidomide, no drugs have been shown to have the effect of preventing growth of limbs.

Acquired limb deficiency is as a result of accident, disease or surgery.

Educational Implications

Illness – Absence of limbs can affect the body's ability to control fluid balance and temperature, since the sweat glands may be missing.

High fevers may develop as a result of minor infections.

Prostheses – Some children are fitted with artificial limbs, which may affect mobility. Additional time may be needed to complete tasks, or to get to lessons.

Practical tasks – Teachers may need to adapt seating arrangements if, for example, a pupil uses his/her feet or mouth to write and perform practical tasks. Technical aids may be necessary, eg a head-pointer to access the computer.

Mobility – Some pupils may use crutches or walking aids. Access and additional time will therefore need to be given. If a pupil uses a wheelchair, access and space is also a consideration.

Pastoral support – Pupils may suffer from low self-esteem, related to self-image. Additional pastoral support will be necessary.

Provision at Stages 1–3

The *Code of Practice* recognises that there are many different causes for a pupil's physical disability and that many children may also have sensory disability, neurology problems and learning difficulties. In addition, some children may experience emotional and/or behavioural difficulties arising from their condition. Differentiation strategies for emotional behavioural difficulties and sensory disabilities are highlighted in other *Spotlight on Special Educational Needs* booklets, but as learning difficulties are so frequently associated with physical disabilities, some strategies for learning difficulties are highlighted in Appendix 1. The list is neither exhaustive nor prescriptive and schools may use any of the following provision and adapt to their own staged approach model.

The provision is linked to four stages: *Stages 1–3* being school-based approaches to difficulties and *Stages 4/5* being equivalent to the stage at which a student has been formally assessed – statement by the LEA.

It would be unwise to attempt to further separate strategies to stages, due to the fact that meeting the needs of pupils with physical disabilities relies so much on individual conditions. As physical disabilities can be progressive and/or regressive, provision needs to be immediate and flexible, according to the ability of the pupil to cope in class. Some pupils cope in mainstream with very few additional resources, while others may require full-time ancillary support.

What follows is an attempt to separate strategies into bands. The first describes all the school-based interventions and the second suggests strategies for pupils who are in possession of a statement of special need, for whom external support may be necessary. All strategies are further explained in the sections on resourcing implications.

PHYSICAL DISABILITIES - STAGES 1–3

STRATEGIES	EXAMPLES
Differentiation	Classroom management ie use of space, seating pupil near exit, near plug for laptop work. Differentiated tasks for PE/practical tasks/school trips, etc. Use of grids/tables to limit amount of writing. Access to computers. IEP Stages 2–4 only written and implemented.
Pastoral support	Identification of key member of staff to give additional support – working with group tutor.
Adapted environment	Handrails, door widening, lowering of switches, temporary ramps.
Adapted equipment	Technical aids ie pencil grips, adapted PE equipment (bats/foam javelin/wristbands for unihoc etc.), keyboard guards, tracker balls, non-slip mats, etc. Vari-height tables/sinks, foot rests, sloped desks, etc.
Curriculum support	In-class support by class/general assistant • for practical help ie in technology/science/art etc. • for curriculum used as amanuensis/reader.
Personal care support	Advice from physio/OT/speech therapist.

Figure 2 – Any combination of strategies for learning difficulties (see Appendix 1) plus.

PHYSICAL DISABILITIES - STATEMENTED

STRATEGIES	EXAMPLES
Differentiation	As Figure 2 plus IEP outlining individual programme based on statement of need, for all appropriate subjects.
Adapted environment	Use of lifts, ramps, separate fire routes. Toilet facilities for disabled students. Rest area.
Adapted equipment	May have personal aids provided by Health Authority ie walking frame, wheelchair, splints, augmentative communication device.
Curriculum support	High percentage full-time ancillary support for lessons ie amanuensis/communicator/reader etc. Special arrangement for exams ie use of amanuensis/additional time etc.
Personal care support	Ancillary support • to administer medical treatment • to help with toileting arrangements • to implement physiotherapy programme • to help with practical tasks eg dressing • to help with meal times. Physiotherapy – advice and/or treatment in school. Speech therapy – advice and/or treatment in school. Occupational therapy – advice and/or treatment in school. GP/school nurse – re: treatment and first aid

Figure 3 – Any combination of strategies employed at Stages 1–3 plus.

Writing Individual Education Plans for Pupils with Physical Disabilities

At Stage 2 or above, the *Code of Practice* requires SENCOs to ensure that an Individual Education Plan (IEP) is drawn up for pupils, which should make use of all resources readily available to the student's teacher. Additionally at Stage 3 or following a statutory assessment, external agency support can be included.

The IEP should set out:

- nature of the pupil's difficulties;

- action taken by the school – provision
  - staffing implications
  - specific details - ie programme/activities/ materials/equipment;

- targets;

- help from parents at home;

- pastoral care/medical requirements;

- monitoring and assessment arrangements;

- review arrangements and date.

The IEP should differ from a pupil's record. It is an action plan, rather than a retrospective record.

LEAs and individual schools differ in their response to the management of IEPs. Some LEAs have a preferred format; however, schools are entitled to develop their own if they so wish. For example, one secondary school has developed an IEP summary sheet (see Appendix 2). In primary schools, one form may be considered suitable for recording all the necessary details of an IEP, but in secondary schools, each subject teacher may need to complete one sheet, outlining targets for their department.

It is anticipated that IEPs will be constantly reviewed to adapt to the school's own method of record keeping and planning.

For pupils with physical disabilities, it may not be necessary to complete details for all subjects of the National Curriculum as *the IEP should reflect the planning which is necessary over and above the curriculum for all pupils.* For example, it may be in practical tasks only that specific targets and equipment are required. In these cases, only a few subject teachers need to contribute to the IEP.

The IEP could be completed as a series of documents, stapled together or held in a loose-leaf file. It should be reviewed each term. The review process may then identify new targets. Suggestions for inclusions in an IEP for pupils with physical disabilities which may be different to other types of special educational needs are provided below.

Nature of Pupils' Difficulties

This section of the IEP may be general or specific. For example, for pupils with physical disabilities, an individual pupil may have mobility difficulties and associated learning difficulties, which affect all areas of school life. Alternatively, a pupil may only require additional modifications in practical tasks.

Schools will also need to consider which terms they may use in this section of the IEP. Norwich (1995) writes about learning difficulties as a term referring to:

- any difficulty which a child brings to his/her learning experiences (these could be better called difficulties in learning);

- general cognitive difficulties in reasoning, perception and memory.

For pupils with physical disabilities, the nature of difficulties may encompass both physical and learning. Schools may therefore need to consider a wider range of implications associated with their education.

Action – Special Education Provision

This section of the IEP is similar for Stages 2 and 3, but additionally includes information and support from external agencies at Stage 3. The plan must make clear what action is to be taken by the school in order to deal with the difficulties outlined.

The action section should therefore detail the provision made by the school in terms of staffing and resources, and should describe specific programmes if they are different to those followed by the majority of pupils.

Examples of details to be included in the 'Action' section are:

- differentiated tasks and materials – eg adaptations to texts, tasks and resources;

- provision of in-class support – ancillary or teaching – number of hours per week specified;

- provision of withdrawal facility for curriculum support – number of extra teaching hours per week specified;

- provision of aids and equipment, and for which subjects/areas;

- provision of physiotherapy/speech therapy/occupational therapy – number of hours specified;

- provision of individual programme – eg a suitably adapted programme for physical education;

- provision of additional time allocated for work and/or exams.

Figure 4 – The 'Action' section of an IEP gives the support to be provided.

Targets

Targets described in an IEP should relate to action and be realistic, achievable and relevant. It will not be possible to achieve all desirable targets in one review period. Rather, a prioritised selection should be recorded for each term.

There is some discussion about how specific targets should be. Norwich (1995) argues that they may be written as:

- specific objectives in observable learner outcome terms, from which specific teaching strategies can be derived;

- sets of related and more general objectives linked to general teaching procedures;

- learning encounters based on general teaching principles, with expected outcomes of only the most general kind.

Figure 5 – Individual students will have their own targets.

It should also be recognised that targets may be achievable over different time scales.

Examples of targets for individual students with physical disabilities may be:

- to increase speed of word-processing to 40 words per minute;

21

- to learn how to use the spell-check facility on the computer;

- to gain a certificate for wheelchair proficiency;

- to learn how to play an adapted form of table tennis;

- to practise working with an amanuensis for larger pieces of writing;

- to swim 10 metres using a flotation aid;

- to use a dictaphone for homework tasks.

All targets should give a time scale by which they should be achieved.

Help from Parents

Schools should work in partnership with parents, and IEPs should specify what help may be required from them, in terms of both practical and emotional support. Such help may include:

- training given to staff who deal with medical and/or personal care treatment;

- support and encouragement to boost pupil's self-esteem;

- regular liaison to keep staff informed regarding progress of child and vice versa;

- support at home for curriculum tasks ie help with homework, practice on laptop, help with practical tasks etc.

Pastoral Care/Medical Requirements

Some students with physical disabilities may require medical treatment, which may require the administration of drugs or, for example, supervising the use of catheters. All schools should have their own first aid and medical policies which specify what treatment, if any, staff may be prepared to undertake and under what conditions. IEPs should outline individual pupils' medical requirements in detail, together with any related school issues for staff. For example, drugs taken by the pupil should be listed, together with regular prescriptions to be taken in school time and their dosage.

It may be useful to describe possible symptoms for staff to be aware of, in case further action may be necessary. For example, if a pupil has hydrocephalus, all staff should be aware of the symptoms of a faulty shunt, so that they can refer to first aid staff if necessary.

Additionally, students with physical disabilities may experience emotional difficulties or may need to discuss personal issues with a member of staff. The pastoral care section of the IEP may therefore describe the arrangement made by the SENCO to accommodate this. Examples of pastoral care may include:

- identification of key member of staff for practical arrangements ie ancillary helper;

- identification of key member of staff for additional pastoral/tutor time;

- withdrawal for pastoral support eg provision of social skills/self-esteem lesson in small group situation;

- provision of individual counselling for sex education – this may be necessary for individual older pupils in addition to the regular sex education received in school.

Part of the IEP for a Year 7 pupil with cerebral palsy is given in Appendix 2. It consists of the technology, English and science sheets, together with a summary sheet. It is given as an example only and is not intended to be prescriptive.

Whole School Approach

In order for successful integration to be achieved, there must be a whole school approach to meeting the needs of all pupils with special educational needs. A school's special educational needs policy should reflect whole school aims. Statements in a whole school policy should include:

- ethos;

- equal opportunities;

- special educational needs policy;

- school organisation.

Ethos
Staff – In order for integration to be successful, the school must create an ethos in which it is believed that *all teachers are responsible for teaching pupils with special needs* and that meeting those needs is not the sole responsibility of the special educational needs department. Differentiation is the responsibility of every teacher. Teaching and learning methods can then be developed which are responsive to individual needs and for different schemes within school. Additionally the attitude of the senior management team is essential to the whole school approach, since their backing and support is vital in ensuring positive action in the use of available resources.

Pupils – In order to develop a whole school ethos of tolerance and create an environment in which all individuals are valued equally, the curriculum should include time to teach students about disability, and working with peers as equal members of the group. Group development work, within a framework of Personal and Social Education, can be invaluable in helping to create such a focus.

Equal Opportunity
The school's equal opportunity policy should include a statement which has a commitment to providing access 'regardless of ability', namely that students with disabilities should not be denied access. The statement of intent for equal opportunities should be agreed by governors, staff and pupils as part of the process of whole school commitment to meeting needs of pupils with physical disabilities. Such a statement would provide the basis for aims in the school's educational policy.

Special Educational Needs Policy
The *Code of Practice* gives guidance as to what should be included in the special educational needs policy (see para. 2:10). The policy should reflect whole school aims and ethos and should outline:

- provision – with reference to physical disabilities it should outline any special facilities which the school has;

- identification, access and assessment for pupils with special educational needs – including integration arrangements;

- staffing – including use of support staff and partnerships with order agencies, links with health services etc.

School Organisation

The values and ethos of a whole school approach are reflected in the ways in which the school groups its pupils. Traditionally, grouping is organised according to the aim of teachers, teaching methods and the needs of the pupils. Mixed ability groups, including pupils with physical disabilities, should be considered in the context of whole school aims. In order for pupils with physical disabilities to be taught in mainstream classes, there should be a variety of groupings including:

- whole class teaching with ancillary help;

- whole class teaching with teacher support;

- small group teaching;

- individual tuition – teacher/ancillary/physiotherapist etc.

A SENCO must be prepared to take a flexible approach to pupils' grouping, so that any or a combination of the above group structures can be included in the provision. For example, a pupil may be able to take part in a maths lesson in a whole class, with ancillary help, but may need individual tuition for a physical education programme.

Structure

If staff are to adopt a whole school approach, then the role of the class teacher or group tutor should reflect this. Pastoral responsibilities should be retained by them, rather than referring to a 'specialist', which can deskill class teachers. Whole school policy should use all available resources to *enable all* teachers to respond to individuals with special educational needs.

Schools should adopt a support network to support teachers in their role. There should be an ethos of shared responsibility, with the SENCO, parents, pupils and all appropriate staff being involved in the planning of provision. An example of this is co-operative teaching, where specialist special educational needs staff work in mainstream classes to support teachers in devising IEPs which are agreed by parents and pupils.

Resource Implications for Provision

Special education finance to schools generally comes from a separate LEA budget heading. It is frequently managed by a separate group of LEA officers. Recent initiatives in budget allocation have delegated funds to schools, resulting in a more flexible approach to provision and resources. Schools must accept the fact that special education students require additional resources and most now take responsibility for managing them effectively. Dessent (1987) argues that schools now need to *redirect* resources, rather than receive more.

> Resources (like needs) are relative. What is at issue here is not the need for more resources (essential as these might be) but the ethical decisions which have to be made about the way in which resources are distributed. If more resources are required, they are required for more children. (page 19)

In the staged approach to making provision for special educational needs, Stages 1–3 are generally resourced from within the school's delegated budget. A flexible approach is required in order to make the best use of the available funds. For example, ancillary staff can be directed to support several pupils in a group, rather than individual pupils, thus spreading the cost.

Resource Implications for Integration

Equipment/Environment

Children with physical disabilities may require considerable adaptations and additions to their environment if they are to lead as independent a life as possible within school.

Guidance has been given by DFEE outlining basic features necessary for disabled students to use school facilities, which includes parking arrangements, ramp gradients, width of doors and adaptations to toilet facilities. All new buildings should now have due regard for people with physical disabilities, but many existing schools do not have such purpose-built accommodation. There are therefore resource implications for the LEA. One possible strategy is to 'cluster' a group of schools in a locality and provide suitable access in one mainstream school, junior and secondary, for students with physical disabilities, rather than attempt to finance adaptations in all schools. However, Male and Thompson (1985) suggest that

> a school which does not meet the standards of the guidance may still be able to cater successfully for disabled students.

The following summarises some ways in which schools can do so.

Adaptations to Buildings

If schools have not been purpose built to accommodate wheelchairs, there are some easier adaptations:

- ramps – ideally should be permanent, but portable temporary ones can be used, as and when required;

- lifts – are desirable where schools are built on levels and stairs need to be negotiated. Stair lifts are an alternative if pupils can manoeuvre themselves out of a wheelchair. (They are generally not suitable for students using power chairs.) If it is not possible to install lifts, then the timetable may be adapted, ie a lesson may be moved from one inaccessible classroom to an accessible one;

- half steps may be purchased for students with walking difficulties, allowing for easier access.

Equipment

There is a wide range of additional aids and equipment available which enables physically disabled students to take part in ordinary life. Ideally such aids should be provided, following consultation with parents and outside specialists (such as occupational therapists). They broadly fall into five areas:

- mobility;

- educational;

- seating;

- communication;

- personal care.

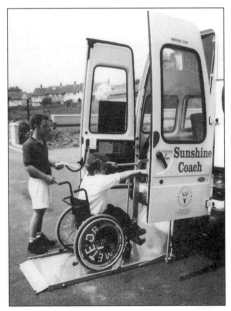

Figure 6 – Aids to mobility will be needed.

27

Mobility

Aids include wheelchairs, crutches, walking frames, splints and adapted boots. These are usually provided through outside specialist and advice as to their correct use should be given to schools.

Educational

Educational aids are many in number and vary from simple aids, such as pencil grips, through to specialist computer equipment. Some typical examples include:

- pencil grips;

- wide-lined paper;

- anchorage devices for paper;

- sloped desks;

- laptop computers (see *Figure 7);*

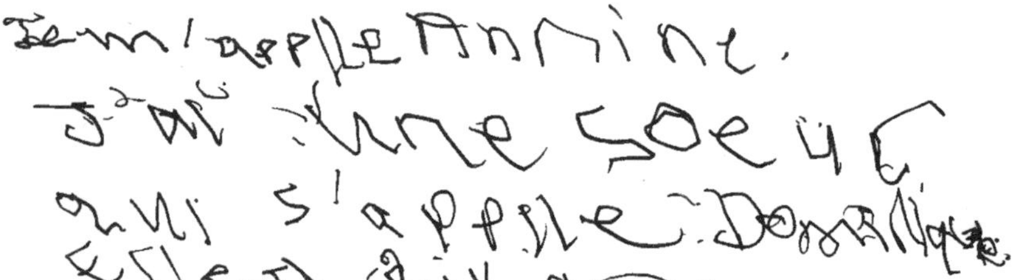

Je m'appelle Annie.
J'ai une soeur, qui
s'appelle Dominique.
Elle a dix ans.

Figure 7 – An example of the benefits of using word processing for a pupil with cerebral palsy.

- keyguards;

- switch access kits for computers – ie single foot switch,
  head switch,
  chin switch;

- tape recorders – using dictaphone to take notes, for example;

- calculators – adapted with large keyboard;

- aids for physical education – eg lighter bats/balls, different shaped balls, velcro bats and balls, foam javelins.

Figure 8 – Many aids are available, including those for PE.

Seating

Pupils with physical disabilities must be able to sit comfortably at a desk at the correct height. It is particularly important that students can place both feet flat on the floor where possible. An occupational therapist can advise on specialist equipment, which may include;

- foot blocks;

- variable height table/desk (see *Figure 9*);

- sloped table;

- seat adjusters.

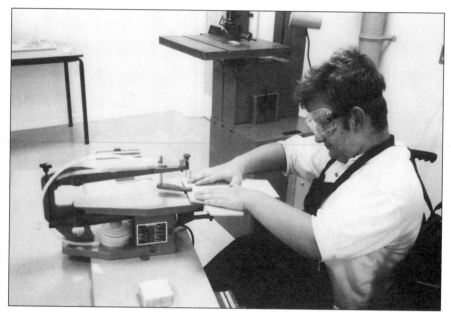

Figure 9 – A variable height workbench.

Communication

Students with physical disabilities may have communication difficulties. For some pupils speech may be developed through regular speech therapy sessions, but for others communication aids may be necessary. These include:

Visual display aids – Boards and displays may consist of symbols, letters or words which pupils point at, using a hand or pointers. Some students may be able to scan and have their own vocabulary book developed. There is a range of boards/display aids available.

Computers – For students who may not be able to communicate clearly, the advances made in information technology allow for written language to be developed. Some software allows for personalised dictionaries to be set up and predict words and phrases with less prompting or typing. Similar versions are available in foreign languages. SEMERC, for example, offers a wide range of software. Advice can also be sought from information technology advisors and advisory teachers, or from charitable organisations working on behalf of people with specific types of disabilities.

Synthesised speech – Computer-produced speech is becoming more advanced and may well be the development that provides access to the curriculum for students with severe communication problems in mainstream schools. Generally, the type of product best suited to the student should be provided following an individual assessment by a recognised organisation such as Augmentative Communication Systems. Referral can be made by a speech therapist. Sophisticated models also allow information to be printed.

Personal Care

Most students, particularly of secondary school age, are independent in their personal care routines and manage with minimum help. However, a small number of pupils with physical disabilities are incontinent and may require extra support. Additionally some pupils may need help with toileting arrangements. Consideration may therefore need to be given to:

A private changing room – Ideally large enough for the student to lie down in. However, alternative rooms may be made available, such as the first aid or medical room.

Changing facilities/equipment – A variable height table is ideal for changing older or large students.

Hoist – There are guidelines in Health and Safety regulations concerning the lifting of people. Ideally, a small hoist should be used to lift larger students.

Equipment – Students should be provided with all necessary equipment by parents, such as pads, bottles etc. It is useful to have a small stock of 'emergency' supplies.

Clothes – Rarely 'accidents' may happen and pupils may need to have a change of clothes available. Although they should be encouraged to provide items themselves, it is useful to have a small supply of 'emergency' clothes available – preferably adhering to school dress codes.

Staff Development

Training

The *Education Reform Act, 1988* outlined the concept of curriculum entitlement as an 'obligation on providers rather than learners'. This implies that mainstream teachers have to deal with a wider ability range than before. They may find that they require additional training to supplement their experience.

Training needs of staff identified in supporting the programme in integration can be identified by analysing job descriptions, evaluating current training and through appraisal interviews.

Training needs for some groups of teachers are more specific than for others. For example, those teachers working with pupils with learning or visual impairment could take a recognised national course leading to qualification status. However, there is also a need for training in general competencies.

Hegarty et al. (1981) found that the majority of teachers working with physically disabled students who felt that they needed additional training, sought two things – more information about physical disabilities and coping with medical conditions; and a better understanding of the educational implications of the disability. In the same study, it was found that teachers reported increased confidence following training and a more relaxed attitude towards students with special educational needs generally.

Proposals for a training programme for teachers should include:

- attendance on LEA courses;

- one – day INSET to develop whole school approach to students with special needs;

- 'twilight' sessions, led by key speakers from organisations such as SCOPE and ASBAH, outlining *educational implications* of physical disabilities followed by synopsis of implication given as hand-outs to staff;

- special needs department handbook for teachers with relevant information about individual students;

- planned programme for new teachers during the autumn term, delivered by the special needs department;

- regular differentiation 'workshops', held by the special needs department, inviting all class teachers to share schemes of work and lesson plans in order to differentiate materials for physically disabled pupils.

Figure 10 – Classroom management is one example of differentiation.

As part of its special educational needs department handbook for teachers, one secondary school has developed a communication and information sheet, known as a 'snapshot', for every pupil with a physical disability. The sheet is filled in by the special needs key worker and is agreed with the pupil. All relevant medical and educational information is briefly outlined, together with suggestions for differentiation. (See Appendix 3.) The snapshot provides some useful guidance to staff on possible strategies for making provision for the pupil's special educational needs.

Resources – Staff

Ancillaries

Ancillary staff are frequently employed to support pupils in mainstream classes, and yet are rarely given relevant training. Some LEAs provide general courses for classroom assistants, but frequently do not offer training in specific disabilities. There are various ways that the SENCO or equivalent member of staff can provide training for ancillary staff, including:

• attendance at any LEA-led courses;

33

- training 'on the job' by more experienced ancillary staff who know the student;

- inclusion in school in-service programmes;

- training provided by the medical staff employed to work in school, ie physiotherapist, school nurse/doctors;

- training provided by parents.

The deployment of ancillary staff needs to be carefully planned by the SENCO in order to make the most efficient use of resources. Ancillary time may be shared by several pupils or allocated to an individual student. Different uses include:

- practical support – assistance with eating, personal care, organising equipment, mobility about school;

- in-class support – acting as amanuensis, help with practical tasks in lessons, specific help with associated learning difficulties etc. (see *Figure 11*);

Figure 11 – Ancillary time can be allocated to one pupil or shared.

- one-to-one support to allow access to mainstream curriculum. This may include support for communication, both oral and written.

It should be noted that training should be offered to *all* ancillary staff, if possible. Problems occur as a result of absences, if only one member of the support team knows how to adapt the curriculum for an individual pupil. It is generally more helpful if the support can therefore be 'shared' by the school's support staff.

Working with Pupils

Schools should be seen to be working in consultation with pupils at all stages of provision. The *Code of Practice* suggests that the effectiveness of school provision may be influenced by the involvement of the pupil.

Pupils should be encouraged to state their views about the effectiveness of provision and to help set targets for their IEP. Some pupils will require guidance and encouragement to achieve this, and a 'critical friend' or advocate may be necessary.

Pupils can be included in the decision making process in the following ways:

- attendance at annual reviews, particularly at secondary age;

- consultation in the evaluation of IEPs;

- consultation and participation in the setting of targets for future IEPs.

Working with Parents

Schools should be seen to be working in partnership with parents. For pupils with physical disabilities, parents frequently supply the initial information regarding the condition, medical needs and daily care of the child. It is worth remembering that most parents will have had several years of experience of dealing with their child prior to him/her beginning attendance at school and often know more about the child than do the staff they consult. Parental involvement at every stage of the school's plans for the pupil is therefore instrumental to a co-ordinated approach. The *Code of Practice* states that:

The relationship between parents of children with special educational needs and the school which their child is attending has a crucial bearing on the child's education progress and the effectiveness of any school-based action.

In the identification and assessment of a pupil with physical disabilities, parents may be concerned about the whole process adopted by the school.

Parents need to be kept informed about all stages of planning and provision made for pupils. Some parents may prefer to be consulted in person, in which case meetings should be arranged in a comfortable atmosphere.

Schools can help parents to work in partnerships by:

Providing information – Information given to parents may include:

- the school's special educational needs policy document;

- local and national contact organisations;

- local services;

- the procedure for assessment and identification;

- the available school resources;

- the names of involved outside agency staff, with contact numbers;

- procedure to deal with complaints/concerns;

- daily home/school diary, where appropriate;

- summary of IEP, where appropriate.

Parental involvement – Parents can be actively involved in the planning process by:

- giving information to staff, eg regarding daily needs, medical care, treatment and progress at home etc;

- contributing to termly reviews;

- contributing to and attending annual reviews;

- contributing to special educational needs department audit and review;

- attending some INSET activities;

- regular contact with concerned professionals, ie speech therapist, physiotherapist etc.

Working with Support Teams

There is a wide range of support available to mainstream school staff, all of which may be called upon to aid implementing and provision for pupils with physical disabilities. Typically, the support services available may come from within:

- the advisory service;

- the psychological service;

- the health authority;

- social services;

- the learning support service;

- the tutorial support/behaviour support service;

- local and national organisations.

Generally, for pupils with physical disabilities, advice and support is sought by staff for *individual* pupils, sometimes through a referral system. There are a variety of ways in which support teams may be utilised by staff in mainstream schools to provide advice, INSET and intervention. The involvement of all support teams should be included in statements and IEPs.

Assistance in Identification and Assessment of Need
At Stage 3 or above, the support may come from the educational psychological service or health authority.

Making Special Education Provision

Schools should always consult social services departments when making provision at Stage 3 or above, and there is a very wide range of support available to schools which help staff to make provision for pupils with physical disabilities at all stages.

Health services and occupational therapists can give advice and resources to adapt existing facilities in class, such as seating aids, posture aids, splints for limbs etc.

Physiotherapists

Physiotherapists give advice on programmes to aid flexibility and mobility. They can provide a programme of physiotherapy on a regular basis and give training to ancillary staff who may implement the programme on a daily basis. Occasionally physiotherapists will give training about the lifting and handling of young people.

Speech Therapists

Speech therapists can give advice and training to staff regarding language and speech development. S/he may also implement a programme on a regular basis in school for an individual pupil. Referrals can also be made by speech therapists to assessment centres, for example, to provide a review on communication devices.

GPs/School Nurses

The school's medical officer, GPs and school nurses can offer assistance in providing knowledge about the medical conditions of some pupils with physical disabilities, together with information about emergency treatment. They may also advise ancillary staff about various medical procedures that the school has agreed to carry out for pupils.

Advisory Services

Advisors may help staff to implement policies in school. They may additionally provide information regarding access to technology and specialist equipment. Training may be provided by the advisory service to teaching staff, either individually or as part of the LEA provision for staff development.

Learning Support Service

The learning support staff may be able to help teachers differentiate work for pupils with physical disabilities who additionally have learning difficulties. They may also provide withdrawal sessions in order to implement individual programmes for literacy. They may advise staff in the purchasing of materials.

Social Services
Some departments in social services are able to offer individual counselling and advice to pupils. Where a pupil has an assigned social worker, s/he can be a positive link between school and home, and aid the school in monitoring the child's progress.

Local/National Organisations and Support Networks
Recognised organisations frequently provide support and advice to parents on request. They may additionally provide INSET to teachers about, for example, the educational implications of disabilities. Some national organisations have referral procedures to assist in diagnosis and treatment.

Within the framework of integration, support services can work in partnership with mainstream schools to develop skills, resources and special expertise. *The Code of Practice* suggests that schools should make service level agreements for such services, specifying scope, quality and duration. This detail, in turn, can be put on the summary of individual pupils' IEPs.

A Personal View

Pupils and parents at Filsham Valley School were invited to write their views on integrating children with physical disabilities. A selection is given below. (Names are disguised for legal reasons.)

A Selection of Parents' Views
Mrs H.'s son has spinal muscular atrophy. He has very little mobility and uses a powered wheelchair. The family immigrated to England two years ago and he was initially placed in a special school for pupils with physical disabilities.

People, in general, tend to assume that if you have a physical disability then you must also be learning disabled, especially if you are in a wheelchair. It is extremely frustrating for a child to be put into a school which is mixing both learning and physically disabled children for lack

39

of sufficient appropriate schools. It is also very frustrating for a parent knowing that her child's potential is not being used.

When my son C. was placed in such a school for one year, he became increasingly unmotivated. There was no educational challenge and few social peers for him to mix with at his own level. Wheelchairs tend to alienate children at the best of times. Without the social aspect of mainstream peers and the intellectual challenge, C. was becoming very withdrawn.

Starting at mainstream in September brought about the usual apprehensions: Will they make fun of me? Can I keep up? Will I get too tired? Will there be someone to physically help me? After the first month it was apparent that this was the best thing for C. He was very happy and enthusiastic about life again. He did his homework with interest. He chatted about his day at the dinner table, children started to come over to our home both after school and on week-ends and after one year he has maintained an average of over 75 per cent in all subjects.

There are so many advantages to mainstream schools for both the disabled and able-bodied child. The challenge, the furtherance of a proper education, the socializing, but also for the able-bodied child. Let them see there is no fear or real differences because another child is in a wheelchair. Let them learn to help with little things like door opening, book gathering, let them form friendships and let the able-bodied child appreciate her or his own good health.

Mainstream school is beneficial to everyone. Hopefully with mainstream integration the next generation will almost wipe out the prejudices and discrimination that the disabled go through.

Mrs H.

Mrs M.'s daughter C., aged 14 years, has a partial depletion of part of a chromosome; a rare condition which has resulted in developmental delay and learning difficulties. She also has diabetes. C. was educated in a special school until 18 months ago.

There are a small number of children who may not benefit from integration in education. However, the majority of children labelled with special educational needs should be given the opportunities afforded to their mainstream peers, being educated alongside them both academically and socially. This in my opinion is the best and only way forward.

Integration should start as early as possible, ideally at nursery age, and continue through to either Year 11 at 16 or, where applicable, college at 18.

The stigma must be removed from all children whether they be gifted, have mild learning difficulties, are physically or sensory disabled or emotionally disabled. All children have problems, so why make special educational needs children conscious of differences by being segregated?

Society, including some teachers, need to be educated to realise the potential and qualities of the children they regard as 'handicapped'. Special educational needs children need to feel worthwhile members of society and this will only happen when they are continually welcomed into all learning establishments.

Mrs M.

A Selection of Pupils' Views

When we first moved to England I had to go into a special school for a year until my new integrated school was built. Now that I am in my mainstream school I am happier because I feel like I am learning something and I also have more friends. People don't talk to me like I'm learning disabled and they treat me like a normal person.

Chris

(Chris has spinal muscular atrophy and uses a powered chair.)

My name is Catherine, I am 14 years old and I think that Filsham Valley School is excellent and the teachers are great because they're so caring towards everyone in the school. I like the work they set us – some of it is hard but I still enjoy it. I like all the lessons we do and we learn a lot of new things in them. My old school wasn't as big as Filsham Valley and didn't have any facilities, like proper science labs, music rooms, PE equipment, assembly hall, dinner hall and art rooms. At Filsham Valley I am taught by subject teachers, who give me any help that I need, and I feel very proud of myself when I get credits and certificates for good classwork. I think that the best thing about Filsham Valley is that the disabled children are involved in all sorts of activities and clubs with the mainstream children and so they become friends. I love my new mainstream school and would hate to go back to a special school where I felt isolated.

Catherine

(Catherine has Wolf Hirshorn Syndrome – diabetes.)

References

Batshaw, M and Perret, Y (1992) *Children with Disabilities - A Medical Primer,* third edition. Paul Brookes: Maryland.

Booth, T and Potts, P (1983) *Integrating Special Education.* Basil Blackwell: Oxford.

Booth, T and Swann, W (1987) *Including Pupils with Disabilities – Curriculum for All.* Open University Press: Milton Keynes.

Department for Education (1994) *Code of Practice on the Identification and Assessment of Special Educational Needs.*

Department for Education Architects & Builders Bulletin No. 77, *Designing for Pupils with Special Educational Needs.*

Department of Education and Science (1978) *Special Educational Needs: Report of the Committee of Enquiry into the Education of Handicapped Children and Young People (Warnock Report).* Her Majesty's Stationery Office: London.

Dessent, T (1987) *Making the Ordinary School Special.* Falmer: London.

Garner, P (1995) in *Support for Learning – a Journal of the National Association for Special Educational Needs.* Blackwell: Oxford.

Haskell, S and Barrett, E (1993) *The Education of Children with Physical and Neurological Disabilities,* third edition. Chapman & Hall: London.

Hegarty, S, Pocklington, K and Lucas, D (1981) *Educating Pupils with Special Needs in the Ordinary School.* NFER–Nelson: Berks.

Male, J and Thompson, C (1985) *The Education Implications of Disability – A Guide for Teachers.* RADAR: Hertford.

Marsh, H, Partridge, L and Youngs, C (1995) *The CAF Directory of Specific Conditions and Rare Syndromes in Children with Their Family Support Networks.*

Norwich, B (1995) in *Discussion papers: II – Schools' Special Educational Needs Policies Pack.* Council for Disabled Children.

Slee, R (1993) *Is There a Desk with My Name on It? The Politics of Integration.* Falmer: London.

Swann, W (1981) *The Practice of Special Education.* Basil Blackwell: Oxford.

Tilstone, C (1995) in *British Journal of Special Education,* Vol. 22, No. 2, NASEN Publications: Stafford.

Further Reading

Dessent, T (1987)
Making the Ordinary School Special. Falmer: London.
This booklet describes policies, provisions and services which facilitate mainstream schools in providing for children with special needs. It promotes debate about 'non-segregation' policies and offers a view about how such a policy could be achieved.

Male, J and Thompson, C (1985)
The Education Implications of Disability – A Guide for Teachers. RADAR: Hertford.
This is a publication of The Royal Association for Disability and Rehabilitation and is aimed at teachers in mainstream schools who have pupils with physical disabilities. Part 1 describes various considerations when teaching physically disabled pupils in mainstream schools, such as education needs, communication needs, social aspects, liaison, design needs and safety. Part 2 contains information about specific disabilities in alphabetical order.

Marsh, H, Partridge, L and Youngs, C (1995) (Editors)
The CAF Directory of Specific Conditions and Rare Syndromes in Children with Their Family Networks.
This is one of a range of services provided to special need co-ordinators. The directory, in a bound folder, provides brief information about a range of specific conditions and syndromes in a form that is easily understood. As a resource to parents, the directory helps put them in touch with others who have been through the same experience. A small subscription ensures that the directory is regularly updated.

Useful Addresses

Ace Centre
Ormond School, Waynflete Road, Headington, Oxford OX3 8DD
(01865 63508).

ASBAH (Organisation for information regarding Spina Bifida and Hydrocephalus)
42 Park Road, Peterborough, Cambridgeshire PE1 2UQ (01733 555988).

Contact a Family
Directory of specific conditions
170 Tottenham Court Road, London W1P 0HA (0171 383 3555).

Muscular Dystrophy Group
7–11 Prescott Place, London SW4 6BS (0171 720 8055).

Nottingham Rehab
A catalogue of aids, equipment and games for the disabled.
Ludlow Hill Road, West Bridgford, Nottingham NG2 6HD
(0115 945 2345).

SCOPE (formerly Spastic Society)
Library and Information Department, 12 Park Crescent, London W1N 4EQ
(0171 636 5020).

Scotiosis Association (UK)
2 Ivebury Court, 323–27 Latimer Road, London W10 6RA
(0181 964 5343).

Simnett Computers
A computer catalogue for educational establishments with a section for
special needs hardware and software, including items from SEMERC.
5th floor, Alperton House, Bridgewater Road, Wembley,
Middlesex HA0 1BR (0800 746638).

Vari-tech
Specialists in special needs furniture.
'Atkinson Engineering', Units 2, 3 & 7, Premier Mill, Begonia Street,
Darwen, Lancashire BB3 2DP (01254 773524).

Responses for each stage

LEARNING DIFFICULTIES

STRATEGIES FOR MANAGING PUPILS WITH LEARNING DIFFICULTIES
AT ANY STAGE MAY BE COMBINED WITH STRATEGIES FOR MANAGING
BEHAVIOUR CHALLENGES AND/OR PHYSICAL DISABILITIES.

STAGE 1

STRATEGIES	EXAMPLES
Differentiated tasks	Varied response to task in place of writing ie cloze technique, cutting and pasting, use of grids/tables, pictorial/oral response, role-play. Simplified task – high quality/less quantity. 'Tiered' levels for tests/exams.
Differentiated materials	Larger text, simplified language, additional illustrations. Homework printed for pupil or scribed by assistant.
Additional time	Extra time allowed for homework/tests.
Access to additional support	Encouragement to attend 'homework help' club, lunchtime and evenings. Staffed by assistants/teachers. Encouragement to attend spelling club, one session per week, lunchtimes. Staffed by SEN teacher.
Monitoring by group tutor	Weekly review of homework diary and discussion re: progress with parents at parents' evening.

© Helen Kenward, 1996.
NASEN Enterprises Ltd.

STAGE 2

ANY STRATEGIES EMPLOYED AT STAGE 1 PLUS.

STRATEGIES	EXAMPLES
Monitoring by SENCO/SEN teacher	Weekly meeting with pupil to establish welfare and progress (informal). Liaison with tutor. Termly review of IEP.
IEP written and implemented	All relevant subject teachers contribute where provision is over and above normal provision for group. Targets specified and strategies outlined. Parents consulted and given summary sheet.
Use of readers where appropriate	Can use ancillary assistants where available, or mixed groups to allow pupil support.
Parental support	Parents invited to contribute to termly review and offer help at home eg reading practice on a regular basis.

STAGE 3/4

ANY COMBINATION OF STRATEGIES EMPLOYED AT STAGE 1 OR 2 PLUS.

STRATEGIES	EXAMPLES
Advice from Learning Support Service	Contact Learning Support Service teacher for advice re: individual programmes/materials etc.
Differentiated tasks	May need to use differentiated levels of work in recognised schemes ie Humanities in addition to those employed in Stage 1.
Support from Learning Support Service	Year 7 only, one session per week individual/small group tuition – withdrawn from mainstream lessons.
Attendance at curriculum support	Withdrawn for numeracy/literacy skills Key Stage 3 for additional teaching.
Use of amanuensis	Work to be scribed following dictation.
Use of reader	Use of reader for end of module tests etc. other than in English.
Access to computer	Could use laptop or networked computer for word processing and spell checking facility.
Access to spellmaster	Availability of spellmaster in class for individual use.

© Helen Kenward, 1996.
NASEN Enterprises Ltd.

STATEMENTED

ANY COMBINATION OF STRATEGIES EMPLOYED AT STAGES 1–4 PLUS.

STRATEGIES	EXAMPLES
IEP written and implemented	Targets written which support needs which have been identified in *statement*.
Curriculum support	Full or part-time ancillary/teaching support to enable student to access curriculum – used as amanuensis – small group teaching – to aid differentiation etc. Special arrangements for exams ie longer time, use of amanuensis, reader, communicator. Provision of laptop for personal use. Provision of spellmaster for personal use.
Withdrawal from some areas of curriculum	May need to be considered if learning difficulties severe eg second modern foreign language in Year 8.

FILSHAM VALLEY SCHOOL
INDIVIDUAL EDUCATION PLAN

NAME:		TUTOR: 7AG	STAGE: 5

SUBJECT: ENGLISH	SPECIAL NEED: PHYSICAL

STRENGTHS & SPECIAL NEEDS:

_____ has a strong imagination and contributes well in class. She has cerebral palsy which affects her speech and ability to write. She is sometimes disorganised.

TARGETS:

- To use a laptop for all written tasks.
- To increase word processing to _____ words per minute (+ date).
- To try to write a little more.
- To retrieve and hand in printouts of work – all lessons.
- To come to lessons prepared with equipment.

PROVISION/RESOURCES REQUIRED:

(Ind. pace, pupil grouping, class organisation, teaching style, staffing, physio, speech etc.)

- One to one with classroom/general assistant(s) – when performing practical tasks.
- Withdrawal for ½ session per week for keyboard skills – general assistant.
- Help with setting up the laptop in class – ancillary or pupil support.
- Reminders from staff re: posture – ie both feet flat on the ground when sitting at desk – class teacher.
- Access to printer in curriculum support area – all times.

SIGNED: .... Teacher.

© Filsham Valley School, 1996.
NASEN Enterprises Ltd.

FILSHAM VALLEY SCHOOL
INDIVIDUAL EDUCATION PLAN

NAME:	TUTOR: 7AG	STAGE: 5

SUBJECT: SCIENCE	SPECIAL NEED: PHYSICAL

STRENGTHS & SPECIAL NEEDS:

C. has cerebral palsy. C. very much enjoys the subject and is a positive influence on the class. She needs to learn to use the computer as an option much more *regularly*. As her condition affects motor control, practical tasks are sometimes difficult for her.

TARGETS:

- To obtain 'standard' grade on the remaining two tests.
- To use laptop/class computer as often as possible.
- To perform all practical tasks, under the supervision of an ancillary helper.

PROVISION/RESOURCES REQUIRED:

(Ind. pace, pupil grouping, class organisation, teaching style, staffing, physio, speech etc.)

- Amanuensis for test worksheets as appropriate.
- Differentiated tests/worksheets as appropriate.
- In class support by me/assistants when experiments are being conducted and she requires help.
- Laptop computer in class.

SIGNED: .... Teacher.

© Filsham Valley School, 1996.
NASEN Enterprises Ltd.

50

FILSHAM VALLEY SCHOOL
INDIVIDUAL EDUCATION PLAN

NAME:

TUTOR: 7AG   STAGE: 5

SUBJECT: TECHNOLOGY

SPECIAL NEED: PHYSICAL

STRENGTHS & SPECIAL NEEDS:

_____ continues to work hard on all aspects of the course. Practical work is always attempted and is willing to try all work and does not give up if there are problems. Her lack of motor control can affect her ability to perform tasks.

TARGETS:

- To maintain current progress to work hard on all parts of the course.
- To use the computer for writing and graphics.
- To perform practical tasks with help.

PROVISION/RESOURCES REQUIRED:

(Ind. pace, pupil grouping, class organisation, teaching style, staffing, physio, speech etc.)

- Support needed for practical tasks – one-to-one/pupil or ancillary support.
- Use of a suitable graphics package.
- Laptop computer in class.

SIGNED: .... Teacher.

© Filsham Valley School, 1996.
NASEN Enterprises Ltd.

51

FILSHAM VALLEY SCHOOL

SNAPSHOT

NAME: | YEAR: 8

NEED TO KNOW:

_____ has a form of cerebral palsy which results in muscle spasm with underlying weak muscle tone. He has extremely immature reflex responses (at last assessment, age 10, those of an 18 month old). He has marked impaired vision in his left eye. His seating is unsatisfactory – OT to be requested. When seated in chair, needs block to raise bottom level so that he can push down through legs/feet to retain seating position. Two people to help with toileting.

EDUCATION IMPLICATIONS:

*   _____ responds with learned responses or by repeating the last option given. The reliability of his statements needs to be checked and double-checked.
*   His sensory system is affected in that he does not pick up information from normal levels of presentation.
*   His seating in both wheelchair and on class chair is slumped unless he is constantly reminded to sit up.
*   _____ is working towards Level 1 of the National Curriculum – requires high level of differentiation.

USEFUL STRATEGIES:

*   When _____ transfers from seat to chair, talk to him about which body part he is moving and touch the leg etc. if he appears stuck.
*   Ask him to sit upright – encourage him to stretch and yawn to open upper body posture.
*   Prepare basic skills curriculum.
*   Record offers and requests for toilet on daily basis.
*   Ancillary support in class.

STRENGTHS:

*   _____ is friendly and appears to be building a friendship with other pupils.
*   He appears happy and pleased to be here.

∗ ADDITIONAL INFORMATION ON FILE ∗

CENTRE LINK: Wendy Lever – Class teacher

© Filsham Valley School, 1996.
NASEN Enterprises Ltd.